Service Recovery

Skills

By

The Customer Service Training Institute

Other Customer Service Training Manuals from The Customer Service Training Institute

Customer Service Basics

Conflict Resolution

Service Recovery Skills

How to Interact with All Kinds of Customers

Great Customer Service Over the Phone

Customer Service for Frontline Personnel

Enhancing the Customer Experience

Customer Service Training for Managers & Supervisors

Customer Service Training for Service Technicians

Customer Service Training for the Hospitality Sector

Customer Service Training for Health Care Professionals

Customer Service Excellence for Security Officers

Safety in the Workplace

How we handle problems can mean
the difference between losing a customer
and creating a customer for life!

Table of Contents

Introduction

Every day even the best businesses strive to make every purchase and every customer contact a productive and pleasant experience. After all, customer satisfaction is the driving force behind every business. Yet, despite the best in intentions, things go wrong. No product is perfect, every service does not go as planned, and no employee or customer is immune from the dreaded "bad day"

Things go wrong. It's a fact of life and we all had better get used to it. It is how we respond to these "unfortunate situations" that is the difference between success and losing a customer.

In this publication we will discuss why some things go wrong and how to respond to these situations. We will also talk about how to minimize these situations and how to turn a bad situation into a good one! (It can be done!)

We will also talk about why we should make these efforts and the repercussions if we don't. Before starting this material, try and think about a few instances where something went wrong and you lost a customer or had serious fallout from the experience. As you go along, try and think how some of the information in these pages could have helped you resolve the situation better. Practical applications will tend to help you remember and apply the material more effectively. Now, on to Service Recovery!

What is Service Recovery?

Service Recovery is the procedure you use to recover from a situation where things went wrong and the customer has suffered. It could be due to a defective product, a missed appointment, or even an honest misunderstanding. Whatever the reason behind the problem, your relationship with the customer, or other party, has changed for the worse. Service Recovery is the efforts expended to repair and rebuild that relationship.

We have all experienced some form of service recovery in our own lives. Remember the time the bakery threw in a few extra pastries because you said the last cake you bought wasn't very good? That's one form of service recovery. We have all been given something off our next purchase because of a problem or inconvenience we just experienced.

That's service recovery. Anything that is done to placate the customer after a problem is a form of service recovery.

As you will soon see, service recovery can take many forms. It can be something as simple as a follow-up phone call or as complicated as renegotiation of contract! Whatever form it takes, it is service recovery!

Why is Service Recovery Important?

In some cases, problems drive customers away. If we don't take steps to minimize or prevent customers from leaving, we run the risk of losing so many customers that our businesses will ultimately fail!

Service recovery techniques help heal the wound to the customer - business relationship. Since it is impossible to eliminate the causes for all troubles, we must respond quickly and efficiently when trouble does strike it's ugly head.

Time is of the essence in service recovery. For efforts to be effective, they must begin as soon after the problem is uncovered as possible. Waiting days, weeks, or months later greatly reduces your effectiveness. Service recovery skills must be implemented quickly.

Service recovery is also has an important financial benefit also. Since it can cost five to ten times more to get a new customer than it does to keep an existing one, service recovery skills do not cost money; they make money for the company!

Another important reason for quality service recovery skills is that you have the opportunity to turn a bad situation into an opportunity. An opportunity to show your customers just how good you are. Those opportunities don't come along that often. If handled correctly, a problem can be turned into a positive experience that can give you a customer for life! That alone is reason enough to implement service recovery techniques!

Stealth Service Recovery

In order to be effective, service recovery must be invisible. Just like the Stealth Bomber, which can't be seen by radar, "stealth service recovery" cannot be obviously noticed by the customer. For example, if you missed an appointment, you would not tell your customer; "I'm sorry we missed our appointment. In order to keep you from going to our competition we will give you a discount off our regular rate for service."

That would seem crass to the customer. You would be much better off phrasing your comments like this: "I'm sorry we missed our appointment. We realize you were inconvenienced and would like to extend a 50% discount to you to show our sincere apologies." This sounds much better doesn't it?

Your service recovery techniques should be presented in such a way that the customer comes away from the experience appreciating the efforts made by your company to resolve the problem. If the experience is positive enough, you may gain a customer that will produce more positive word of mouth advertising than you could ever imagine!

Example: My wife and I take our children to Walt Disney World every other year. We usually spend about ten days on the premises and have a wonderful time. One year, we booked a plan including admission tickets and hotel accommodations. We arrived late afternoon and wanted t see the last performance of the Electrical Parade before the parade went to Europe. Much to our dismay, no one had our tickets and the ticket offices were closed for the day. We were told to go to the park and explain our situation and see what could be worked out.

We went to the park, explained our situation to the Customer Service person and he offered us 4 free passes for that night! Needless to say, we were very happy. Good customer service so far, right?

When we returned home I wrote a letter stating how pleased we were with the way the incident was handled. I also stated that keeping ticket counters open in the hotel would have eliminated the frustration that we felt when we arrived. I did thank them again and mailed the letter.

A couple of weeks later a letter arrived from the company. It contained a letter of apology and 4 seven day admission tickets worth approx. $750.00!! The note of explanation stated that they did not want any visitor to experience frustration when they came to their parks. The hoped we would use these tickets and come back to give them another chance! Needless to say, we were thrilled.

A couple of weeks later we received another letter containing a check for the tickets that we purchased for our trip. I thought that there must have been a mistake and called their offices. I was told that there was no mistake. They had made an error that resulted in us having less than a wonderful experience and they wanted to refund our money!

Needless to say, we were extremely impressed with the treatment we were given. It far exceeded anything we expected! We were so impressed that we went again the next year instead of waiting the extra year!

This is a perfect example of excellent service recovery. For those of you that think this cost the company a lot of money, let's look at it from the company point of view:

The largest expense was the cash refund. That came to about $750.00. That's a bottom line figure. The actual cost of the 4 free tickets? Since the parks would be open anyway and all the rides operating, the only actual cost of the tickets was the few pennies it cost to print them! Add a couple of dollars for postage and that's about it! With that in mind, let's take a look at what the company gained from their actions:

We used the free tickets and went the next year. We probably spent $2,000.00 during our time there! That's income to the company they would not have had if we did not get the free tickets. I figure that we are about even now. Here's where the company really gets the benefit of their actions.

Over the course of the last few years I have told countless family and friends about this story. I have used this example in seminars and printed material such as this publication. All this free publicity has been achieved by a simple, yet presented in an extremely effective manner, gesture of good faith by the company. It is impossible to figure the value of that kind of word of mouth advertising!

The unique thing about the above example is that the service recovery was presented in such a way that we were drawn to return and give them a second chance. Not because we really deserved all we were given, but rather because we were made to feel that we really were appreciated by the company involved. We were being asked to give them another chance to let them shine. The best part of it all was that it was all wrapped up in a package that generated some revenue for the company at the same time! As you will learn later, this was a perfect example of a win-win situation!

No matter what method of service recovery you choose, it is critical that you present in such a way that it is not obvious to the customer that you are doing this just to retain them as customers.

While some will see through your methods, most will be happy to be treated with respect and dignity!

Where Service Recovery Starts

Service recovery starts the minute the customer walks through your doors or calls you on the phone. Service recovery starts before the purchase has even been made! How is that possible?

One of the major tools used in service recovery is the reputation of your company and it's employees. If your company has a reputation for producing high quality products and services and standing behind them when they fail, you efforts at service recovery will be easier. If you have a poor reputation, you may find yourself dead before you even start!

Reputation buys you the benefit of the doubt. If you buy a name brand product and it fails to do what it is supposed to, you may try it again. If you buy an off brand product and it fails, you may say "It's my fault for not buying a name brand. I'll go out and buy a name brand now." Same exact problem, very different reactions.

Take the time to develop a good relationship with your customers and gain their respect. A good reputation is worth more than all the advertising in the world. The perception that your customer has of you and your company will influence every situation that may come up in the future.

Service Recovery is also dependent on the quality of your products and services. No amount of good intentions will compensate for a poor quality product or a service that does not live up to its claims. While no product or service can be perfect all of the time, you must strive to produce products and services that exceed the expectations of your customers. Only then can you expect any Service Recovery effort to succeed.

Any business owner will tell you that the only way to succeed in today's economy is to keep existing customers happy while adding new customers on a daily basis. Your efforts to keep existing customers happy through quality products and proper service recovery efforts will enable you to create a reputation and environment that will draw new customers to your business.

A Better Way to Look at Problems

Suppose you found yourself losing customers every day without knowing why. How do you think you would feel about that? What do you think you would do? If you are like most of us, you would look at your business an try to identify what the problem was. You could spend days, months, even years trying to identify just what the problems were. In the meantime, customer loss would continue. This seems like sure-fire recipe for failure.

Now let's look at the same situation from another angle. Your customers come in and complain about your products, services, or business practices. They voice their displeasure and threaten to go elsewhere in the future. Their visits are unpleasant and sometimes get downright ugly! Some customers do leave and never come back.

Which scenario would you prefer? If you are serious about the long-term success of your business, you should have picked the second example. Why? The truth of the matter is that the second example gives you a chance to salvage your relationship with your customer before they leave for the competition!

In order to achieve success in Service Recovery, you must alter the way you view and respond to complaints. **From this point on, you must view complaints as opportunities!** People who complain are giving you valuable information on what they don't like about you and your business! They give you a chance to respond to their complaints. **Complaints give you a chance to show your customers just how good your business really is!**

Complaints can furnish you with information that you may never have discovered on your own. Maybe your product does not function well when used in a specific application. Perhaps people just don't understand how to use a certain function of your product properly. Maybe your instructions are confusing or contain mistakes. Whatever the reason, your customer has a problem that you may never discover yourself no matter how hard you try! The information in a complaint can save you hours and hours of needless work and efforts!

Let's say you are a company that produces computer software. One of you most successful products has a bug in it that causes a certain type of computer to "crash" when the program performs a specific action.

If your customers complain about the problem, you can get valuable data. What kind of system is it? What kind of software do you have on it? When did it crash? What specific functions were you using? What error messages were generated?

This information let's you detect and remedy the problem quickly. It allows you to identify the problem and solve it so that future users do not have the same problem. The information provided by the customers narrow down the problem to small areas of the program. This reduces the time and efforts needed to identify the problem areas.

What would happen if you didn't get the complaint? You would not know that the problem existed. You would keep making the same product with the same flaws and new customers would get a defective version. You might spend time and effort looking for problems in products that don't exist. You may think there are problems in areas of the company that are working just fine! You would lack any information that could lead you down the right path to finding the real problem.

I strongly suggest that the next time a customer calls or visits you with a complaint or problem that you thank them for bringing it to your attention. Sincerely thank them. Act like they just gave you a check for a thousand dollars! Do this because the have given you something far more valuable.

They have given you information that will help you increase customer satisfaction in the future. They have given you direction to soling a problem. They have also given you a chance to restore your company's reputation.

The best time you greet that angry customer, than him for the opportunity to listen to them voice their displeasure. There's a lot to be learned by listening.

Knowing the Value of your Customers!

It is easy to underestimate the value of a customer. This is especially true in businesses where the amount of the average purchase is just a few dollars. As we underestimate a customer's value, we tend to minimize the need to take steps to make these customers happy.

Our minds treat things according to the value we place on them. We are more apt to take good care on an expensive item than we are a cheap, throw away piece. Think for a moment. If you were offered $20.00 to do a job, you may feel it is not worth the time or inconvenience involved. If that same job paid $1000.00, you would think a little bit more about your decision. The same goes for your customers.

It is important that you realize just how much each of your customers is worth to your business. When you can accurately understand their value, you will find yourself treating them very differently.

A very common misconception is that the value of each customer is equal to the amount of his or her last purchase. For example, if a customer buys a quart of milk from you for $2.00, then the value of that customer is $2.00. In reality, the value of that customer is far greater.

When we talk about the value of a customer, we must take into consideration the amount of purchases, the frequency of purchases, and the anticipated amount of time that customer will make those purchases. After taking all these factors into consideration, we can arrive at the true value of that customer. Below are a few examples:

1) A customer buys a quart of milk for $2.00 twice a week. The value of that customer should be $4.00 per week, $208 per year, or $2080 over 10 years!

If you do something to anger that customer, the loss to your company over time would be over $2000!

2) A customer buys a copy machine for $500.00 and a one-year service contract for $200.00. The average life of the copier is 7 years. The cost of 7 years of service contracts is $1400.00. The copier will also use supplies worth $250.00 per year. The cost of supplies over 7 years will be $1750.00. Therefore, this customers worth to your company would be $500 + $1400 + 1750 or $3650!

These figures do not include two very important factors that cannot be accurately measured. Those two factors are the amount of additional business or purchases over and above their normal purchases, and the amount of referral business that they are responsible for.

Referral business is additional business that is generated by the positive comments or recommendation made by your customer. For example, a current customer recommends your business to a few of his friends that he knows are in the market for your product or service. This referral will only occur if your customer is happy with your business.

The amount of referral business can be staggering. You never know whom your customers will be talking to about your company. One recommendation can be worth thousands of dollars in business! Good news also travels fast. One person tells another, who tells another, etc. Though it is impossible to trace future business back to an original referral, it is not uncommon to have referral business that far outweighs what your original customer may purchase themselves from your business! Here are a few examples:

1)   A person buys a roast beef sandwich for lunch at a local deli. The meat on the sandwich is of very poor quality. The person returns to the deli and asks for a new sandwich. The deli refuses. The cost to make the sandwich is $2.00. What can the bad sandwich cost the deli in the long run?

Let's say the average person buys lunch out twice a week and spends an average of $5.00 per lunch. That's $10.00 per week or $500.00 per year. This same customer works in an office with several other people. Let's say he tells two of his co-workers about the experience. They do not wish to get the same kind of treatment so they go to another deli for their lunch. Two people at $500.00 per year equals $1,000.00. The office also caters ten business lunches a year. Each lunch costs them $250.00. The quality of the food is important so, after hearing of the bad experience, they choose another business to cater the lunches. The amount of this business $2,500.00. The total loss of business would be $4,000.00! Four thousand dollars of lost business because of a sandwich that costs $2.00 to make!

2)   Mr. Hubbard attends a local business club luncheon at a local conference center. His food arrives and it is barely warm. He asks the waiter to take the food back and heat it up. The waiter takes the food, and instead of re-heating it, prepares an entire new entree and serves it to Mr. Hubbard along with an apology. The waiter also returns a few minutes later to make sure the new entree is satisfactory.

A few months later, Mr. Hubbard's company is considering potential locations to hold their national meeting. He remembers the excellent treatment he received from the waiter at the convention center and recommends that location.

The convention center gets the weeklong meeting along with the over $30,000 in business it generates. The convention center gets this meeting for the next 5 years. Total business generated, $150,000! Cost of satisfying the customer? An entree and a few words.

The above two examples are conservative in nature. They are designed to demonstrate just how much money and business may possibly be won or lost depending on how you treat a customer.

In addition, note who was involved in both examples. A deli clerk and a waiter. Front line people! No one in management was responsible for either customer experience! These two examples clearly show the power and influence customer service people can have in business!

Never Under-Estimate

the Value of a Customer!

All businesses have certain customers that are treated differently than the rest. The customers buy large amounts of product or maybe recommend your products or services to their clients. Their purchases or recommendations represent considerable business for your company. When these customers want something, you tend to do everything in your power to accommodate them.

In the building trades, these customers may be large developers. In retail business, it may be a large chain of stores. In a specialized industry it may be one company that purchases all of your product! (Like the company that sells McDonalds it's french fries!)

Whatever the situation, you tend to do whatever you fell is necessary to insure that your company retains their business.

That's only common sense. Here's something to think about, however. When the next customer walks through your door, how do you know his or her importance?

In the second example you just read, the gentleman with the bad entree did not give any clue to the waiter as to his job or of a possible referral for future business. He was just an ordinary man with a problem. A problem that just happened to be solved in an exceptional manner.

There will be many instances where you will come into contact with customers that could have a considerable influence over those people that deal with your company. It is not possible for you to know who all these people are. You may know who an important client is but do you know what his or her spouse looks like? We all know what our boss looks like but how many of us know what our bosses parents look like? If we did, I'm sure that we would treat them just a little bit differently, wouldn't we?

The point that I am trying to make is that we should establish a minimum level of service that we provide to every customer that walks through the door. That minimum level of service should be at a level where no one could feel that he or she was not considered important to your company.

As previously stated, our minds tend to treat people and situations according to the value we place on them. If we learn to view every customer as a potential referral for a major new account, you will find yourself treating all your customers just a little bit better.

Why Do We Need to Know the Value of Our Customers?

You may be asking yourself why we need to know the value of our customers. After all, if a customer has a problem, we need to solve the problem and provide a resolution to the customer regardless of his or her worth. Essentially, this is true. However, in business, decisions are always based on a cost vs. benefit basis. This means that whatever action a business makes, it must bring in a value that exceeds what it costs. This helps insure profitability.

Value does not always mean cash. Value might be in the form of referral business, publicity, and other tangible items.

Examples of value would be donating goods or services to a charity in exchange for a banner or ad in their yearbook. In this case, the cost of the goods is less than the potential benefits of the advertising.

Only when we understand what a customer truly represents to our company, can we determine what courses of action are appropriate. The greater the value of the customers, the more you can spend resolving their problems. For example:

Mr. Ryan purchases a tool for $129.95 from a local hardware store. That is the only purchase he has made in 10 years. The tool breaks just after the warranty expires. The tool manufacturer refuses to extend the warranty. Mr. Ryan demands you give him a new tool.

Mr. Smith purchases the same tool and has a similar problem after the warranty expires. Mr. Smith buys all of his hardware from you and also purchases substantial materials for his business also. His purchases total about $10,000 per year. He also wants a new tool.

In the first example, furnishing a new tool to the customer would result in losing money on the transaction. Since this is not a regular customer, you would be hard pressed to justify this course of action. The value just is not there. In this case, you might explain the warranty to the customer and offer the customer a discount on a new tool or perhaps another brand tool. This would show a good faith effort on your part.

The second example might be treated differently. This customer purchases a considerable amount of products from you each year. The cost of the tool can easily be recouped in future business. By providing a new tool you cement your future relationship with this customer and help insure his continued patronage.

As previously stated, it is impossible to know every single person that does business with your company. You cannot possibly know who has certain contacts in your industry or who knows who. Because of this, Service Recovery must establish certain guidelines for all customers. I prefer to use the following rule of thumb: **If the cost of a solution is less that the original profit from the sale, do it!**

Let's use the following example:

Mr. Jones buys a tool for $100.00. Your cost is $40.00. The tools beaks just after the warranty is over and he requests a new unit at no cost. If you feel that making this customer happy may lead to more business in the future, you could give him a new tool and still have a $20.00 profit on the transaction. You would still have made money on the original transaction. On the other hand, if you feel that little or nothing would be gained by making the offer, you could try to offer a discount or other token good faith offer.

Reality vs. Perception

What is the difference between doing a poor job and doing a good job your customers perceive as poor? NOTHING! The harsh reality is that there is no difference between perception and reality when it comes to your customer's view of your business.

It has been said many times in business that you need your customers but your customers don't necessarily need you. Unless you are a sole supplier of a certain product or service, your customers will have other choices of vendors. They may exist just fine when dealing with another company but you cannot survive without customers!

Here is the single, most important, reason for Service Recovery efforts:

Your customers have the right to do business with whomever they choose. They have the right to patronize the business that they feel provides the best service. They also have the right to do business with whatever organization they feel addresses their needs on a continual basis.

Not only must you work hard to produce the best product and service that you can possibly produce, you must also create an impression in your customers mind that you are the best vendor for that customer. You must create a positive perception in the eyes of your customers.

The key to creating this perception lies in the following:

• **Be the best you can be!** In order to create a positive impression, you must have "your act" together! By being pro-active and continually refining internal policy and procedures, you will limit the number of bad experiences that your customers will encounter. By giving your customers good experiences, you will create a feeling of confidence and trust.

• **Don't downplay a negative experience!** It's a common mistake to not take some problems seriously. There are two hidden dangers in doing this. First, if you give your customer the impression that you do not care about his or her problem, no matter how small it might be, you run the risk of losing that customer forever. Second, a negative experience stays with a customer for a long time. It might take 5 or 10 good experiences to negate the effect of a single bad experience. Worse yet, you may never get the second chance you need to prove yourself to the customer.

- **Accept responsibility for the error.** If you made a mistake, ADMIT IT! Take the steps to correct it and assure your customer that this is not a normal occurrence. If you try to pass the blame off on someone else you will run the risk of appearing less than honest with the customer. NOTE: If you did not make any mistakes, be careful what you may admit to. There may be legal repercussions to your statements.

- **Take credit for good things!** If you give a customer something that they are not entitled to, let them know in a nice way. This accomplishes several things. First, it lets the customer know that you have an honest desire to make them happy. Second, it let's them know that they are getting something that they are not usually entitled to and that they should not expect the same thing in other situations. This allows you to resolve the issue without setting an unreasonable level of expectations. Lastly, letting the customer know they received "above the line of duty" treatment will insure that you are not held to the same offer when similar situations arise.

- **If you're good, LET PEOPLE KNOW!** If you do something better than your competition, tell people. Put it in your advertisements, include it in your literature, make it part of your sales pitch. By letting your customers, and future customers, know your strengths, it creates a positive perception in the minds of others. That's basically what advertising revolves around! Why do people pay more for a name brand? Because they have the perception that the quality is better than other brands. Is the quality better? It might be but the important thing is the perception of the customer.

- **Guard your integrity!** The most important thing a business has is its integrity. If something should happen to damage that integrity, the results could be disastrous. When you are in a situation with a customer, do the right thing. Never take an action that could come back and damage what you have tried so hard to create. Stand behind your products or services, support them as promised, and treat your customers well.

- **Defend your company's image.** We all have an image to uphold. With an individual, it is the image of being a good mother or father, or maybe that of a good and trustworthy person. With a business, it is an image of honesty, professionalism, and customer service. If something should happen to damage that reputation, we must respond. If a competitor says they are better and they're not, don't let it go unchallenged. If a competitor spreads untruthful information concerning your company, fight back. We are talking about perception. Sometimes, the truth can become altered by the way something is presented. If you don't believe this, just think about some of the political commercials you see on television. Both sides claim they have the best record and have statistics to back it up. They use different words to suit their purposes. Defend your image and your reputation. It is the only way to insure that your customers, and future customers, get the correct perception of you and your company.

• **Promote your strengths and learn from your weaknesses.** Never rest! Always look for ways you can improve. Learn from your problems. They let you know what to improve! Recognize your strengths. Play on those strengths to create the best image possible. Always keep you eyes and ears tuned to your industry. Never be caught napping while others pass you by!

• **Don't go for the "quick fix."** A good reputation can take years to build and minutes to tear down. A positive perception is something that is built up little by little over time by way of experiences, comments from others, and other tings that alter the way we see things. Negative experiences and comments carry more weight with our minds than positive experiences. Because of this, a single negative experience can negate the results of several years' worth of work. Strive to resolve internal and external issues with solutions that will insure that these issues will not be a factor for many years, or ever again. Short-term fixes will come back to haunt you time and time again. Take the time to do things right.

Many of us are unaware of the power of perception. Perception alters the way we look at a business, person, or place. It helps determine our initial views and opinions. Our perceptions form a baseline for you actions and reactions.

Let's say you purchased a product and spent extra to buy the best brand possible. You did your research, picked out the product you wanted, and settled on a brand name. You buy the product and you have trouble shortly after the product is purchased. The product is serviced promptly and works fine afterward.

How would you feel toward that product. Your initial feeling would be disappointment but you would have a certain level of faith in the company that manufactured and sold the product. That faith was validated by the fast and professional service. You would probably buy from that company again.

Now, same product, no-name brand. Same problem, same service done in the same time frame. Would your feelings differ?

You would probably feel that you should have bought the brand with the better reputation. Your faith in the product, as well as your decision to buy it, will have suffered. Next time you probably will think long and hard about buying the same brand again. Why do you think that is?

For years we have been conditioned to buy by name. We have drilled into our heads on a daily basis that such and such brand is better than brand X. Our minds start to form a perception that this is true because we hear the same message over and over again. Repetition creates a perception in our minds. If we follow this perception, we feel our actions are validated. If we deviate from this perception and experience problems, we feel that we are partially at fault. The comfort level is just not there.

Why do you think people spend billions of dollars every year on name brand cars, windows, hotels, and other items? Because **the perceptions we have developed allow us a certain degree of security and comfort.** We feel comfortable buying certain products. We feel comfortable dealing with certain companies. **The bottom line is, if your customers can develop a feeling of comfort, trust, and security in dealing with your company, you will have a customer for life.**

A positive impression of your company in the eyes of your customers will often help you resolve issues and problems more easily and with less expense. A feeling of security and confidence will tend to minimize the effects of a negative experience. A common way to express this would be to say that you would receive "the benefit of doubt" from your customers.

Unfortunately, the exact opposite is also true. If your customers have a poor perception of you and your business, they will tend to find fault and displeasure at every stage of the problem or issue. In more common terms, you will be "damned if you do, damned if you don't."

As you can see, the perception your business has in the community or industry can have a profound effect on the success or failure of your company. This perception is the result of many years of hard work and quality products and services. Guard this perception closely. Do not allow it to become tarnished, damaged, or destroyed. Take whatever steps necessary to restore it after a problem or incident. In it's basic form, Service Recovery is also Perception Recovery.

Creating a Service Recovery Action Plan!

Just as a general would not send his troops into combat without a battle plan, you must also create a plan that will guide you, and your employees, along the right path. This plan will help insure that everyone plays by the same set of rules.

You might be asking yourself why an action plan is necessary. Why not just treat every situation as it comes and make a decision to make the customer happy? That is surely easier than creating a plan and making that plan available to everyone.

The problem with that approach is that everyone is going to treat the same situation differently. Two people with exactly the same problem could be offered two different solutions. If these two customers happen to compare notes on what they received, you might have trouble brewing.

For example, customer A has a product that is defective. She speaks to operator A and is told to send it in for repair. She does this and is happy. Later she talks to her friend who had the same product with the same defect. That person talked to a different operator, let's say operator B, and was sent a new product along with a 50% discount coupon off a future purchase. How do you think the first customer will feel now? Not very good.

Often problems will require more than one phone call to resolve. In cases like these, it is very possible that your customers will talk to more than one person in your company. In these cases, it is critical that everyone makes the same statements and the same offer to the customer. If this is not done it creates confusion and frustration in the eyes of the customer.

An action plan greatly reduces these problems by establishing a clear set of guidelines that are used by everyone in the company. If you encounter a certain situation, you are to offer no less than A but no more than B. These guidelines also speed up the Service Recovery process.

Establishing a set of guidelines allows a person to make a decision on the spot without having to delay the process by getting someone else to approve a particular course of action. History has shown that the faster an issue is resolved, the less costly the solution will be. In addition, customer satisfaction goes up when the resolution time frame goes down.

A good Service Recovery Action Plan includes the following items. You actual plan may include more than what is listed below. The following items must be included in even the most minimal action plan:

- Organizational Flow Chart
- Overall description and philosophy of the program
- Human Resource and Cost Analysis
- Hiring the Right People
- Policy and Procedures
- Escalation Procedures
- Internal & External Communication policies
- System checks and balances

We will now discuss each of the above in detail. Keep in mind that each application will be different and that you may have to adapt the information to fit your particular needs. The principals and ideas behind the information should remain intact.

Organizational Flow Chart

It is important that every person in the company knows who performs what function in the company. Very often, a question will come up and it will be necessary to know who to go to in that situation. An organizational flow chart provides that information.

The flow chart should show area of the company. This includes Management, Administrative, Financial, Manufacturing, and all other areas of the company. Under each area, a contact person should be assigned for the purpose of assisting in the Service Recovery efforts. For example, under the heading "Accounting" would be listed "Ann Roberts, X.2343" When a question involving the accounting department comes up, you would look on the chart and see the contact name and phone number.

Avoid the temptation of just using a generic phone number for a particular department. It is far more effective to assign one or two people to handle these customers. The reason for this is simple. When you have a problem, the customers involved are usually somewhat unsettled or annoyed. By designating a specific person instead of an entire department, you can control who has access to these sensitive customers. By using this approach, you can direct your customers to employees that are experienced in dealing with these types of situations. They can then proceed to diffuse the situation and resolve the issue in a timely manner.

The one thing that you never want to have happen at any stage of the recovery efforts is to have sensitive situations handled by new or poorly skilled employees. An organizational chart can help limit those situations.

Your organizational chart can also be used to guide an employee to the correct area to route angry customers. For example, it is commonplace for customers to ask to speak directly to the President of the company. By using the organizational chart, you can direct the customer to the correct individual. Let's say a customer asks to speak with the President of the company. In the organizational chart, an entry listed under the President's office would indicate "Customer Complaints to be transferred to Tom Wright, Assistant to the President X2345. This information allows a person access to the correct person for that particular situation.

Depending on your individual application, your company may require more than one organizational chart for Service Recovery purposes. Your company may produce products under more than one brand name. In that case, it is not unusual for different people to handle problems for different brands. In cases like these, each chart must be clearly marked and designated for the proper application. If many such charts are used, a directory sheet, explaining the use of each chart, should be included to help the person determine the suitable chart for that particular situation.

Organizational charts provide vital and correct information to the people who deal with your customers. Their sole purpose is to assist in moving the customer to the right people, in the right order, to reduce the time it takes to resolve the issue.

As previously stated, the faster the issue gets resolved, the lower the cost to the company.

Let's take a moment and think about what might happen if we did not have such a chart. A customer calls up and asks a question. They are transferred to a person that says, "I don't handle that, you want Jim in shipping." You speak to Jim in shipping and he says, "That's not a shipping issue, you want Mary in the order department." You talk to Mary and she says, "Wait a minute, you need to talk to Herb in sales." When you talk to Herb, he sends you back to Jim in shipping!

This particular course of action spells doom for your company. First, it creates the impression that your company doesn't know what the heck it is doing! Secondly, it allow the anger and frustration level of the customer to go through the roof! Thirdly, it increases the time required to resolve the issue. The second and third reasons combined make it much more expensive to satisfy the customer if you even can at this point!

Your actions on the phone, and in person, and your ability to provide the right information to the customer control the outcome of every situation. If you can show that you are efficient, accurate, and professional in dealing with your customers, you will help in creating that positive perception. If you show just the opposite, the result will be a negative perception.

Philosophy and Description of the Program

Do you think it is possible for an employee, or individual, to make a decision without knowing the needs and goals of the company?

In order to be effective in their positions, people need to have a purpose and a set of values by which to judge their actions and options. Without these needs and goals, people will lack in direction and motivation.

Different companies will have different sets of reasons for implementing a Service Recovery Program. For some, the main drive will be customer retention. Others will use the program as a sales tool. The overall success of the program can only be achieved when all parties involved have a clear understanding of the purpose of the program.

We should take a moment and talk about customer retention and service recovery as a sales tool. In the most basic form, all service recovery programs are geared towards customer retention, customer satisfaction, and long term profitability. The difference between using the program as a sales tool and using it just for customer satisfaction is the lengths the company will go to make the customer happy.

While the two philosophies are similar in nature, the decision making process uses two different thought processes. Customer Satisfaction requires that we offer solutions to problems in relation to the cost of the products they purchased.

Using service recovery as a sales tool will include current purchases as well as the value of anticipated future purchases from high volume customers. Since all resolutions have a cost associated with them, it may make sense to the company to offer higher cost options to those customers that represent large future purchases. The philosophy of the two focuses is similar but use different thought processes.

People need to know the priorities of the programs they participate in. Only when they know the desired end result can they make decisions that they feel are correct for that particular situation.

Program descriptions are also important as they provide a "feel" for the program and will guide the participants down the desired path to service recovery. As with any program that involves multiple participants, it is critical that everyone projects the same image and follows the same policies and procedures. A program description helps deliver the right message to all involved.

Human Resources and Cost Analysis

In order for any new plan or procedure to be successfully implemented, it must be established up front exactly what resources are required. Resources include staffing, equipment, office space, printing and forms cost, etc. All these costs must be established in order to assure an orderly start to the program.

Very often, the top one or two people in the existing service department or middle management do service recovery. In these cases, it is only necessary to establish just how much time these existing people will devote to the service recovery efforts and whether or not other existing duties must be reassigned to make that time available.

In other cases, new personnel must be hired to perform these functions. When this is the case, there are several factors that must be addressed. These factors become part of the Human Resource and Cost Analysis plan. These factors will include, but not be limited to, the following:

How many new employees will be needed?

How long will it take to train these new employees?

What will their level of compensation be?

What skills are needed for each position?

Whether existing employees are transferred into the new positions. Or new employees are hired, there are other questions that must be addressed:

What are the specific job descriptions for each position?

What is the reporting structure for the position?

What is the established salary and benefit package for each position?

What specific background and/or qualification are required for each position?

This is just a few of the questions that should be answered. For more questions and specific information, consult a Human Resource professional.

Other costs such as space, equipment, printing, and supplies must be estimated to insure sufficient start-up funds are available. Keep in mind that you may need a year or two to accurately forecast the volume of work that you will need to handle. Ideally, Service Recovery efforts should reduce the amount of complaints your company receives. Fewer complaints means lower workload which means less expenses. All these factors must be considered when planning out a Service Recovery operation.

There is one more very important reason for this type of plan. Any program that relies on the input and judgement of others must involvement every participant. Studies have shown that people become more involved, and more productive, when they are made to feel that they are part of the program and not just employees of the company.

Customer Service is different from any other kind of service. Words, emotions, and communication skills are the tools you will use to solve problems. There are few black and white issues.

Almost every situation requires judgement and creative thinking. Because of this, your success will be directly attributed to just how much your employees desire to satisfy the customer.

In Service Recovery, we routinely "Go the extra mile" to satisfy a customer. We bend rules, give a customer something for their trouble, and make efforts to win back that customer. This requires more than someone just putting in their eight hours and going home. To be successful, you must have people that care. Making your employees part of the process helps them to achieve that level of commitment and become a team player.

Hiring the Right People

The single most important factor in the success or failure of a Service Recovery plan is the quality and skills of those people charged with carrying out the plan. Hire the wrong people and even the best plan will fail and fail quickly. Hire the right people, and the plan will succeed and what problems do arise will be minor in nature.

A recent survey asked people what they look for in a service person or customer service person. The most common answers were, listening skills, being on time, inspires confidence, courtesy, compassion, and job knowledge. Note that only one of these items requires technical skills. All the other items require basic customer service skills.

What do you look for in a service employee? You can't go by education, no one gives a degree in Customer Satisfaction. What you need to look for is someone that can meet the following criteria:

Good Communications Skills - Since the bulk of this job will be dealing with customers on a daily basis, communications skills are the single most important skill for customer service people. Candidates should be able to express themselves easily and clearly when talking to a wide range of people.

Appropriate Appearance - If the position requires direct face to face contact with your customers, it is important that every employee has an appearance that is appropriate to the industry he or she works for. Appearance depends on the industry. For example, if you were going to invest $100,000 and you went to a financial advisor that was dressed in jeans and a T-shirt, you would not be overly impressed. If you hired a plumber or carpenter, however, that same dress would be entirely appropriate.

You will hear some people say that appearance has nothing to do with the skill level or competence of the person. That's absolutely correct. No argument there! What appearance does have an effect on is the perception (there's that word again!) that the customer has of that person when they first meet!

How confident would be of a weight loss product if it was being sold to you by someone that was 350 pounds? Probably not very confident. The appearance is not appropriate to the situation.

In service, your focus should be placed on an appearance that tends to inspire confidence and calm your customers down. If your appearance puts your customers at ease, you have won half the battle.

Hire people who are self-confident and relaxed

Don't let anyone kid you. Customer service is not for the weak at heart! Customer Service requires a mixture of self-confidence and self-control. In order to be successful you need to be relaxed and confident in your abilities to make the right decision and then stick by it.

Customer Service is also no place for nervous or high-strung people. Remember that the ability to get your customer to feel relaxed and comfortable is a very important part of the job. If your people are nervous and hyperactive, this will tend to increase the anxiety level of your customers.

One very effective way to identify the correct people for the job is to hold a longer interview than usual with the applicants. Get them to talk about themselves and other things other than the job or company. See how they portray themselves. If they can talk and communicate in a relaxed and calm manner in that situation, that is a good sign.

An interview is a very stressful situation. The applicant feels somewhat intimidated and has something to lose if they give a poor "performance". If someone can be relaxed in this type of situation, chances are they will be relaxed in the work environment also.

Another undesirable trait is talking too fast. When talking with customers, or any person for that matter, you want the conversation to be in a relaxed tone and atmosphere. If a person talks very fast, the other people involved in the conversation may miss some of what is being said and may even totally misinterpret what was said. In addition, the anxiety level of the other party may rise dramatically because he or she just can't keep up with the conversation.

Self-confidence is also important because people involved in Customer Service must make decisions on a moment's notice. They must evaluate the situation, take all factors into consideration, and make a decision. Then they must be strong enough to stand behind that decision and implement it.

If you should have a person with little or no self-confidence, that person may hesitate to make a decision, or refuse to act on their decision without getting that decision approved by someone else. This increases the time required to resolve the problem and adds to the frustration level of the customer. Customer Service people must also be confident enough in their abilities that they can stand behind a decision they know is right and not be intimidated into changing the proposed resolution by an over aggressive customer.

On the other hand, there will be cases where someone will make the wrong decision. It may be that important information was not available when the decision was made and now this new information changes things a little. A secure and confident person will not hesitate to admit to the mistake and will take steps to correct his or her actions. An insecure person may stick to their original position no matter what because they see change as admitting defeat.

Experience

It is difficult to put someone into a customer service position without any background in the product or industry you are involved in. That does not mean that you must have direct industry experience to be effective.

A background of service or customer service is very helpful. Previous experience as a technician, repair person, clerk, bank teller, and any other positions that require direct customer contact is relevant experience. Unlike technical skills, customer service skills are readily transferable from industry to industry.

The skills used to resolve an issue in a department store can also be used in a car dealership, food store, medical office, and other customer service situations. Any experience of this kind should be considered a positive.

Technical skills are another matter. If you are involved in a Service Recovery operation that involves technical products or specific technical knowledge, these skills must be present for the person to be effective in their job.

For example, if you service computer products, the customer service people must have a basic understanding of industry terms, jargon, and equipment operation. This information is needed to understand and identify customer problems and concerns. In these kinds of positions, former technicians with customer service skills may be good candidates. This is especially true if your salary structure makes the customer service position a higher paid position than the technicians.

Policies and Procedures

Your policies and procedures book is the blueprint for your entire Service Recovery program. It provides every employee with a specific path to follow when dealing with customers. Included in the policy and procedures book will be:

- A description of your warranty and enforcement guidelines.
- Procedures for filing warranty claims.
- Procedures for filing non-warranty claims.
- Situation specific information.
- Special situation procedures.

A description of your warranty should be included so that everyone in the company knows and understands exactly what is and is not covered by the warranty.

The warranty should be worded clearly and made as black & white as possible to avoid different interpretations. Your goal here is to make sure everyone reads, and interprets, your warranty the same way. We want to present a unified appearance to our customers.

Every company has procedures for handling warranty claims. Do you return the unit to the factory or send it someplace local? Does your company pay for shipping costs? What is the anticipated turnaround time? What paperwork is required and who is the paperwork sent to? What address does the customer send the product to? If the customer has to pay part of the costs does that amount have to be paid up-front or will the company bill the customer? All these questions, and more, should be answered here.

These same questions, and others, should be covered for non-warranty products as well. Every company has different policies and all these policies should be outlined here.

Very often there will be common, yet specific, situations that will arise. Perhaps it's a common known defect which the company wants handled a specific way. It might be a n application error that the company has a specific solution for.

Whatever these situations might be, any specific course of action should be outlined here so that every employee is aware that there are ways for these situations to be handled.

Always remember that the intent is to have everyone act the same way, and present the same message, to your customers in the same situation.

Escalation Procedures

Escalation is a crucial part of the Service Recovery process. Basically stated, escalation is the process of transferring a customer to another party that can help resolve the issue. Usually it is a person with more authority but, in some cases, it can be someone of equal or lesser authority. We will talk about escalation in detail later.

It is important that everyone knows to whom he or she should be transferring their customers. Transferring your customers to the wrong people adds to the frustration level of the situation. It also makes you look less than professional in the eyes of the customer.

Your escalation procedure should contain two basic flowcharts of escalation. The first is the management escalation flowchart. This flowchart indicates the sequence of escalating a conflict through the management ranks. This is used when all efforts to resolve the situation have failed and the customer demands to speak to a manager or even the President of the company. The sequence would be something like, clerk, supervisor, assistant manager, manager, vice president, assistant to the president, president.

The reason for this is simple. When a customer demands to speak to the president of the company, he or she does so for effect. They do not expect to speak to the president. What they do expect is to get someone in management to address their concerns. The president of a company is far too busy to take calls from individual customers unless it is a very critical problem.

The escalation procedure will give your employees the correct sequence to escalate a problem. When followed carefully, very few calls, if any, will make it to the vice-president or president.

The second flow chart will resemble an organizational chart. This will list all the departments and a designated person in that department that will handle all problem calls. With this type of chart, the correct person can be contacted to speed up the resolution process.

The sole purpose of these charts is to provide easy to find, accurate information to speed up the resolution process. If possible, these charts should occupy no more than one page each. When the charts are one page each it is easy to scan the entire chart rather than look through pages of data.

Internal & External Communications

In most situations you will have internal people you will interact with such as co-workers, warehouse people, sales people, and other on-premises personnel.

You will also have external people such as suppliers, vendors, distributors, etc. To insure success in customer service you must establish a policy for communication between these people.

Contact names must be made available for all departments and external vendors and distributors. It is important that all written and verbal communications reach the correct person. While this may be similar to the escalation flowchart mentioned previously, there is one difference.

Some communications will contain information about problems and suggested changes to the product or system. These types of communications will usually be sent to the management of that company or department. Internal and external communication lists will often identify both a management contact and another contact for information and problem resolution. It is then up to the individual to identify the correct person for that situation.

We will discuss the importance of communication later. For now, let's develop a list of correct people to contact.

Checks & Balances

Even the best-laid plan will develop problems. Changes that evolve may reveal hidden problems or short comings that need to be addressed. Because of this, you must include a system of checks and balances to insure that your program continues to function well and address the needs of your customers.

Checks and balances are just a fancy name for monitoring. You want to monitor your program to make sure that people are doing what they are supposed to be doing and that the correct results are being obtained.

Monitoring can take on many forms. Monitoring of phone calls is a form of monitoring just how well your people talk with customers. Everyone has made a call and heard "To insure customer satisfaction, this call may be monitored for content." This is one of the checks and balances.

Surveys are another form of monitoring. A performance meeting where people from different areas of the company meet on a regular basis to discuss service is a form of monitoring. Follow-up phone calls after problems are resolved is another example.

Checks and balance are critical to the long-term success of any project. Just as conditions in the marketplace change, so do your customers and their needs. Your competition changes on a daily basis. You must also. A good system of checks and balances will prevent you from getting that dreaded comfortable feeling.

Checks and balances should be established and put in writing. Being up-front about what is being done will greatly reduce any feeling of "big brother is watching" paranoia that may exist with the employees. Another benefit is that if people know they are being monitored, they will be just a little more careful of what they say and how they act with your customers!

The information presented so far should give you the basics on how to design, set-up, and prepare an effective Service Recovery system. Now we will discuss just how we will handle problems that arise with customers, retailers, distributors, and other people we will deal with on a daily basis.

Methods of
Service Recovery!

You've got your plan together, hired your staff, and have more problems to handle than you can shake a stick at! You've got an angry customer on line 1, a screaming lady on the selling floor, and a stack of complaint letters on you desk that could choke a horse! I think this is a great time to start doing what we've been gearing up for!

We are going to take you through each step of the service process, explaining what has to be done and why, the resources needed, and the consequences of not doing the job right. While some information may be repeated from time to time, that information is relevant to the topic being discussed. Using this format, it is possible to read just one section at a time and not have to look back through other pages to find out certain information.

This works great when you need to brush up on just one part of the process.

Stage1: The Initial Contact!

The initial contact occurs when the customer, or other party, first makes you aware of a problem or concern. This contact will usually be made to an employee at the retail or service level. Usual contacts will be clerks, sales people, receptionists, operators, etc. Initial contacts do not usually go direct to upper management.

One very common mistake is to ignore the importance of that initial contact. Despite the fact that the people involved at this point are not corporate level decision-makers, their conduct will set the tone for the entire experience. Because of this, it is critical that these employees be equipped with the required customer service and communication skills to do their jobs.

Let's examine a first contact. A customer has a problem with a product they just purchased. They return to the store and approach the clerk at the retail counter. That clerk is busy talking to a friend and ignores the customer until finally the customer interrupts their conversation and asks for help.

The clerk does not hide her annoyance and tells the customer to get a new one off the shelf and bring it to the counter. She resumes her private conversation. The customer gets the new product, brings it to the counter, and hands it to the clerk. She puts it in a bag and hands it to the customer without saying a word. The customer leaves with his new product.

What do you think the reaction to the customer will be? He should be happy, right? He got a new product, didn't he? Of course he did! So why should he have anything but a positive feeling about the experience?

The sales clerk did several things wrong and didn't do some things at all. Let's examine what happened or didn't happen:

1) **No personal greeting or acknowledgement** - The clerk should have acknowledged the presence of the customer and terminated her personal conversation immediately. If she were talking with another customer, she should acknowledge the customer by saying something like "I'll be with you right after I'm done with this gentleman" or "I'm busy at the moment, let me get someone to help you". Both of these statements acknowledge the presence of the customer and reduce the stress level of the situation.

2) **She kept the customer waiting and waiting** - Your goal in service recovery, or customer service in general, is to get the situation resolved as quickly as possible. This means responding to the customer quickly, assessing the situation quickly, and providing a timely solution. In the above example, the clerk made the customer wait until the customer's patience was gone and he interrupted the conversation between the clerk and her friend! At that point, do you think the stress level had gone up or down?

Studies have shown that the faster you can resolve an issue or situation, the less expensive the resolution will be. The longer you wait, the more it is going to cost you to resolve the problem.

3) **NO EMPATHY!** - When someone comes to you with a problem, express empathy for the customer and his or her situation. A simple, "I'm sorry you had a problem with that radio Mr. Reynolds. Let me get you a new one right away." gives the customer the impression that you are sorry that he or she had the problem. It gives the impression (or perception!) that you care about your customers. Total elapsed time to show empathy, five seconds! Effort required, little!

Showing empathy further reduces the stress level of the situation. The more you can reduce the stress level of your customer, the easier it is going to be to effectively communicate with him or her.

NOTE: Do not confuse empathy with acknowledging responsibility! Do not say anything that will imply any admission of guilt or responsibility. That could come back to haunt you if the matter reaches legal stages. A simple "I'm sorry you had a problem" will usually suffice and be harmless. In any case, follow the guidelines established by your company for acceptable phrasing and procedures.

4) **NO direct assistance** - Instead of telling the customer to go to the shelf and get a new unit, the clerk could have gone and picked up one for the customer. If situations prevent the clerk from leaving her location, at the very least she should have said "please" when asking the customer to do something.

The easier you make it on the customer the better off you will be. By doing as much for the customer as possible, you can control more of the resolution. Maybe the customer will come back with the wrong unit and have to go back again. That will irritate him some more. By making the customer do as little as possible, you increase the enjoyment level of the experience and stand a greater chance of satisfying that customer.

5) **NO CLOSURE!!!** - The clerk just placed the item in a bag and handed it to him while carrying on a conversation with her friend! The clerk should have placed the item in the bag, thanked him for his patience, and asked if there was anything else she could help him with.

This accomplishes two things. It provides the store with another opportunity to express their regrets for the problem and it also brings "closure" to the problem.

Closure is a term that means bring the experience to an end. Closure helps to assure the customer that nothing else needs to be done. It lets the customer's mind process the fact that everything is done and the matter is closed.

A closing statement also provides an opportunity for the customer to ask any remaining questions he or she has. If the customer has any other expectations, they will be brought out at this point.

The need for closure may seem a little ridiculous to you but it is a very valid concern. In some companies, as many as 10% of customers still feel that something else is going to be done while the business involved has considered the problem resolved.

Unresolved issues are a major problem in Service Recovery. We have talked a little about fast resolution. Unresolved issues can go unresolved for months. Think about what can happen to a frustration level over that period of time!

6) **Lack of respect!** What do you think the clerk showed to that customer? Her actions showed a total disregard and a lack of respect to the time and needs of that customer. The above example was easy to resolve. A new unit was given to the customer and the matter was closed. The actions of the clerk, and the disrespect she showed him, probably cost the store a customer.

It must be noticed at this point that all the errors mentioned above were all customer service skills. No special technical knowledge was required. The cost to resolve the above problem? The cost of the product. The cost of the lost customer? We may never know!

Now let's look at the same example handled just a little bit differently. A customer walks into a store with a defective radio. A clerk greets him as he walks into the department and asks if he could be of any assistance. The customer shows him the defective radio. The clerk says, "I'm sorry you had a problem with this. Let me get you another one off the shelf. If you could go to the counter over there, I'll be right with you." The clerk gets the radio and brings it back to the counter. The clerk takes the new unit out of the box, plugs it in and tests it. "I wouldn't want you to have to come back again so let's test this one out now", the clerk says. It works, the clerk boxes it up, puts it in a bag and asks if there is anything else he can do for the customer. The customer says he already sent in the warranty card for the original unit with the serial number on it. The clerk tells him that there is no problem. Simply return the new warranty card with a note about the change and the warranty records will be changed. The clerk then thanks the customer for his understanding.

What happened this time?

1) **A greeting was made** - Before the customer could get to the counter he was approached by a clerk and was offered assistance. The result? A reduction in the frustration level. The matter is being handled quickly and effectively.

2) **Empathy was shown** - The clerk voiced his regret for the problem. Further reduction in frustration level. The customer also gets the perception that this business cares about their customers.

3) **Assistance was given** - The clerk went and took the radio of the shelf. He even went as far as to test the new unit out to make sure that it worked properly.

4) **Closure is achieved** - By asking if there was anything else that he could help with, the clerk provided closure. It also gave the customer the opportunity to raise the question of warranty coverage.

5) **The customer was thanked** - By thanking the customer; you instill a good and positive feeling with the customer. Customers do not want to feel like they are burdens or inconveniences. They want to feel appreciated. Thanking a customer gives them this feeling.

6) **The customer is reassured** - By taking the time to test the new radio, the clerk has assured the customer that the new one is working fine. This starts the healing process of the experience and helps to restore faith in both the store and the product. In addition, by taking the time to address the concern about the warranty, the customer will leave the store with a secure feeling about the future operation of that product.

With this second example, we have accomplished several things. First of all, we have made the customer feel important and have demonstrated that we are concerned for our customers and their business. We have provided the customer with a positive experience to help offset his negative experience. We have also addressed his concerns about the future and long term reliability of a product that he just had trouble with.

Compare the two experiences. The second experience took a few minutes longer (most of that time was testing the unit, which will not happen all the time) than the first example. The end result was that the second example resulted in a happy and satisfied customer while the first example resulted in a lost customer. The cost to resolve the issue (except for time involved) was the same. The end result was very different.

The initial contact is crucial because it can set the tone for all future conversations and action.

If you had to talk to that same customer if the problem could not be resolved, would you rather follow experience #1 or experience #2? The obvious answer is number 2. The second situation has left a very positive impression on in the mind of the customer. He or she is likely to purchase from you again. Do you think the customer in the first example is likely to buy from you again? Not likely!

Every effort must be made to make the first contact as positive as possible. One important reason for this is cost. Generally, positive experiences reduce the amount of costs it will take to resolve a situation. Negative experiences increase the costs of resolving situations. The reasoning behind this is simple.

If you are treated well by someone or some company, you will tend to develop confidence in the people you are dealing with. You will accept their ideas and offers more readily and with more confidence. If this confidence is missing, you will tend to ask for more from the individual to help compensate for the lack of trust.

The human mind always strives to be in some kind of "comfort zone". A comfort zone is where your mind is at ease and confidant. You will have a feeling of security based on previous experiences. You are confident in your ability to handle the present situation.

In service recovery, we want to create this "comfort zone" as quickly as possible.

Stage 2:

Creating the "Comfort Zone!"

As we previously stated, a "comfort zone" is a feeling in your customers mind that makes them feel at ease and receptive to communication. This "comfort zone" is where meaningful communication and dialogue take place.

If you have every tried to talk to anyone when you are angry and upset, you will probably recall that little was accomplished in that conversation. In fact, there was probably more lost than gained. Heated debates and arguments rarely accomplish anything positive. Instead, they usually increase the costs of resolving any issue. In some cases, they may make resolution of any kind impossible.

In contrast, when people carry on conversations in a relaxed manner, most conversations will result in positive actions and solutions to the problems.

When talking in a relaxed state, people are more receptive to negotiations and listening to the actual content of the conversation. The are few, if any, "walls" between the people involved. Conversation is constructive, or neutral in nature. Situations that are not resolved are usually made better as a result of the communication.

Creating this "comfort zone" is not as difficult as you would imagine. All that needs to be done is to use some basic customer service skills. Use your skills to reduce frustration levels. We have already talked about this. Get to the customer quickly, acknowledge his or her problem, listen, and take steps to reassure the customer. As the frustration level reduces, you get nearer to the comfort zone.

Most of the time you will get involved in a service recovery situation, the situation will be negative in nature. It may be a mild irritation or a full-blown anger that you are confronted with. No matter what the situation, your first efforts should be to get your customer back to a neutral state. Don't try to solve the problem all at once. Diffuse the anger and try to get to the neutral state. The neutral state is where you have the anger eliminated but the customer does not necessarily feel anything positive. Neutral means not positive or negative in nature.

If the situation is being handled face to face, such as in a retail environment, try and move the site of the conversation to a private area. This accomplishes two things.

First, it does not let other customers hear of the problem the customer is having. Second, people tend to be more reasonable when they are not in front of a group of people. When other people are present, the person may feel a greater need to be firm and unyielding. They may feel a greater desire to "win" in front of others. They want to make themselves look big and important in the eyes of others.

The key to creating a comfort zone is **building trust**. If you can convince the other party that you sincerely want to help them, you will open the door for a positive impression and a creation of the comfort zone.

Building trust requires a series of positive actions, comments, and impressions. Each action or comment helps create a positive image of you in your customer mind. As this positive image increases, so does its power to influence your customers thinking. Your customers comfort zone will start out very small and grow with every positive experience. The stronger it grows, the more confident your customer becomes. The more confident your customers get, the easier it is to communicate with them.

It is critical that everything your customer experiences is positive in nature. Studies have shown that one single negative experience can have more effect on your customer's confidence than 6 - 10 positive experiences.

We have talked about the need to have everyone apply the same rules and procedures as everyone else.

Allowing people to act independently is one sure-fire recipe for disaster. Make every effort to make every act, comment, or impression positive in nature.

Remember we are still talking about that first contact. During the first contact, the importance of positive actions is the greatest. Why? Think about what we have talked about so far. We talked about building a comfort zone. How is that comfort zone built? It is built on the actions and impression that have happened to that customer. The more positive experiences, the stronger the comfort zones.

If a customer has a negative experience early in the service recovery process, there are few, if any, positive experiences to offset the negative one. Recovering from this bad experience will be very difficult, or maybe even impossible. Later on in the process, a negative experience, while it will hurt the chances of resolution, may have several positive experiences to limit its power. We do not have this luxury early in the process.

Greet the customer nicely and quickly, acknowledge their problem, create the impression that you honestly want to help them resolve the issue, and diffuse the frustration and anger level. Get to the neutral point and attempt to develop a level of trust between you and the other party. Don't try to rust this process. If you give the impression that you are trying to rush things along, the other party will not think that you are really interested in helping them. Trust will not be developed in this situation.

Stage 3: Listen, Listen, and Listen!

Some of the most effective and important things you do will revolve around your ability to listen to what others are saying to you. Listening allows you to gather important information that you will then use to resolve situations more easily and in shorter amounts of time.

Effective listening requires several skills. They are:

Not talking while others are talking.

Don't interrupt others while they are talking.

Asking the right questions

Separating words from emotions.

Identifying important areas of concern.

When you go to the doctor, does the doctor come in, write you a prescription, and send you home? Of course not. The doctor will ask you what the problem is and then ask you questions designed to narrow down the problem to a specific point. Service Recovery uses the same approach.

When a customer comes to see you with a problem, let them explain the problem to you. Even if you know what the problem is from experience, let the customer explain it to you. This accomplishes two things.

First, it allows the customer a chance to "vent" their frustrations and anger. This is important because it helps to reduce the frustration level of the situation. (Remember that we want to get to that neutral point.)

Secondly, it also gives you specific information that lets you either confirm or change your diagnosis of the problem. Always keep in mind that the desired end result is not for one party to win but rather for both parties to arrive at an acceptable resolution to the problem.

If at all possible, do not interrupt the customer while they are talking. This will tend to increase the frustration level and eliminate the chance for the customer to vent their frustrations. Instead, let the customer continue and act with patience. Unless the customer shows no signs of ending, and starts to ramble on, spend the extra few minutes and let the customer talk.

Asking questions is a powerful tool we all use every day without realizing it. When we sit down to watch TV and ask what channel the game is on. The answer allows us to get to the right channel without searching through the other 9,543 satellite channels until we get to the right channel! Ask a question, get an answer. It is a powerful tool if you learn how to ask the right questions.

Service recovery and identifying problems use a series of questions with the intention of narrowing down a problem to fewer and fewer causes until we are reasonably assured that we have the right answer. The more questions we ask, the more we can narrow down the possibilities.

For example, let's say we need to identify a number between 1 and 50. If we ask, "Is it 37?" and the answer is no, we have only eliminated one possible answer. We would have to ask up to 50 questions to get the right answer!

Instead, we would ask, "Is it more or less than 25?" If the answer is more, we have eliminated numbers 1-25. If the answer is less, we have eliminated the numbers 25 to 50. Your next question would be designed to further reduce the number of possible answers. If you are dealing with 26-50, your next question would be "Is it more or less than 37?" Ask more questions until you have narrowed down the possibilities as much as possible.

In many cases, you may not have the ability to pinpoint the exact cause with 100% accuracy. In these cases, you should attempt to get as much information as possible and then make an informed decision.

You decisions are only going to be as good as the information you have at your disposal. Asking questions, and listening to the answers, will provide you with a wealth of information to use.

There are also going to be instances where emotions will govern the words used by a customer. In order for you to be effective, you will need to recognize this and separate the emotions from the words.

Emotions result in phrases like; "This piece of junk is useless! It does work now, it didn't work when I bought it, and every product you ever produced is junk too!" Is there any relevant information in that statement? Aside from the fact that the product does not work, not much else. Let the customer vent their emotions and them try to get back to that neutral point. Reassure the customer, ask specific questions aimed at reducing the number of possible causes, and resolve the issue. Diffuse the emotions; don't let them govern the situation.

It is very important that you respect the emotions of your customers. Whether these emotions are justified or not, always remember that you are there to satisfy the customer. These emotions are part of your customer and must be addressed also.

Many times during a conversation, you are going to recognize information concerning the real problem the customer has. It may concern a spouse, previous experiences, or an underlying fear or insecurity in the customer's mind. It is important that you uncover this information when it is given to you.

Generally, if you hear a certain point over and over again in a conversation, that point has a special significance to that particular individual. That point is preventing that person from entering their "comfort zone." If you can address that specific point, you stand a good chance of being able to resolve the issue in a satisfactory manner. If you fail to address that point, you will never arrive at a solution that satisfies the customer.

For example, a customer comes in and says, "I bought this product from you last week. I had to drive 65 miles to buy it and now I have to drive back because it doesn't work. It's obviously defective and I want to know what you are going to do about it. I don't want to make this trip again. It's 65 miles each way you know."

This customer is dissatisfied for two reasons. The first is a defective product and the second reason is that he had to travel 65 miles each way to return it to the store. We know the travel distance is an issue because he repeated it twice in his statements. Identifying this as an issue will determine how you present a solution to the problem. An effective way of dealing with this situation would be as follows:

"Sir, I'm sorry you had a problem with this unit (acknowledge the problem and express empathy), this has been shown to be a very reliable unit but even the very best products can have a bad unit slip through. I will exchange the unit for you right now. (This resolves the defective product issue.) If you should have any problems in the future, you can mail the unit to our main office and we will take care of any problems. (This addresses the travel concerns and fear of problems in the future.) We will even reimburse you for the shipping costs. Here's our office phone number for your records." (This relieves fear of paying shipping costs and the phone number gives the customer security if problems arise in the future.)

In the above example, both concerns were addressed. The customer now feels confident in the way his problems were addressed, accepted, and resolved. The person involved took the time to listen to the customer, identified his concerns, and uncovered a hidden concern. The person addressed all these issues and found a solution that made all parties happy.

Listening also addresses one last, but still very important issue. It demonstrates a degree of respect for your customer. By taking the time to listen to what the other party is saying, you impart the feeling that you have respect for that individual. You show the other party that you have a sincere interest in resolving the issue correctly. You also help build that positive experience and increase the size of that person's comfort zone."

Stage 4:

Arriving at Solutions-

Balancing the Customer

vs. the Company

Wouldn't it be easy if we could just give every customer what he or she wanted without concerning ourselves about the costs involved? Satisfy every customer; give everyone everything they want. Everyone leaves thrilled. Talk about a perfect experience!

The problem with this approach is that you and your company would soon be bankrupt! Every decision must have a sound financial basis in order to be effective.

Give everything away and the costs will quickly bury even the most financially sound company. If you give away too little, the customer will walk away and never buy from you again.

What needs to happen is that a middle ground be established so that the needs of all are addressed in a fail and equitable manner.

Service Recovery efforts take into consideration several factors. We look at the value of the customer, the cost of each possible resolution, and the possible future ramifications of our decision. All three must be taken into consideration when deciding on the best resolution.

Often there will be several possible resolutions to a particular problem. Standard practice is to present the least expensive solution first. If that is acceptable, great! You have resolved the issue in a very cost-effective manner. If the solution is not acceptable, then you would present the next alternative and then the next and so on. The idea is to rank possible solution from the least costly to the most expensive and present them in the order.

Care must be taken with customers that purchase large amounts of product from you. You do not want to run the risk of insulting them with a low-ball solution when their purchases entitle them to better treatment. This is why we have talked about knowing the value of your customers.

When considering possible solutions, you must also take into consideration any legal requirements that may be involved. Warranties for example, give a customer certain specific legal rights, which must not be denied. For example, if you warranty states the customer is entitled to a replacement unit, you should not offer to repair the unit.

If the warranty states a specific entitlement, you must abide. You have the option of offering more than what is entitled but never less.

No matter what the customer or situation represent, never start off by offering the best resolution. If you should give the best resolution first, you have no room to negotiate. It is human nature to negotiate for something more than what is initially offered. If someone can get a little more through negotiation, it gives the person a positive feeling and leads to forming a positive impression and creation of that all important comfort zone. By always leaving something to negotiate, you have the ability to increase the offer should you decide that is what is required. Leave yourself options.

Stage 5: Presenting the Resolution

You have talked to the customer, asked the right questions, identified all the issues involved, and have uncovered several options to resolve the problem. After you have done all that, you need to switch hats and become a sales person.

It is now your job to "sell" that customer on a specific course of action. How do you go about selling this resolution?

The first thing you have to do is ask yourself if you feel the solution is fair. If you don't believe in it, there is no way you can effectively present it to your customer. Most people will see through a phony presentation. If you can convince yourself that the proposed resolution is the way to go, then you can proceed with confidence and sincerity.

Every solution has features and benefits. Features are the meat of the resolution.

An example of features would be: replacement of a unit, refund of money, repairs, free shipping, extended warranty, etc. Features are what the offer is made up of. Features are designed to address issues and resolve the situation.

Benefits are what the features of the solution represent to the customer. Convenience, confidence, reliability, insurance, and economy are examples of benefits. Benefits are what the customer is looking for in the resolution.

When selling a particular course of action to a customer, you will need to know what the problem is and how to address these concerns by identifying the benefits.

In the example of the gentleman that traveled 65 miles to return a defective product, one of the benefits of the solution should include the benefit of convenience. Let's use that example again. To refresh your memory, the customer has a defective product and has traveled 65 miles each way to return the unit.

We have offered a new unit and given him the ability to mail the unit back next time with reimbursement for postage. In this example the features and benefits of the offer would be:

- **Feature** - Replacement of the defective product. **Benefit** - addresses the issue of the defective product.
- **Feature** - Offer to ship unit to factory in the future. **Benefit** - addresses concern over 65 trips in the future. Builds confidence and reduces worry.

- **Feature** - Reimbursement for postage costs. **Benefit** - eliminates costs for future problems. Builds confidence and reduces worry.
- **Feature** - Providing Main Office phone number. **Benefit** - provides avenue to address future problems. Helps build confidence and indicates willingness to satisfy customer now and in the future.

Whenever you need to sell something to someone, always concentrate on the benefits the other party will receive from that course of action. The reason for this is that some people may not understand all the topics your proposed situation represents. By presenting each benefit one by one, you let your customer understand the full value of the solution.

Another important reason is that the more positive images you can present to your customer, the more receptive your customer is going to be. Remember when we talked about perception? We stated that perception is the result of many experiences, items, and statements made to that person. By presenting benefit after benefit to the customer, you are layering one positive experience on top of another, each one helping your customer to accept the solution you are proposing!

Take a moment and think about the last time you went to buy a large-priced item. It might have been a car, home, or even a big screen TV. How did the sales person sell you that unit? Let's use a home as an example.

When the real estate agent showed you a home did they say, "Here it is? You want to sign a contract?" If they did, you wouldn't buy it! Instead, the sales person listed the benefits of this house over other similar houses. "Look at the view of the lake and the large closets in the master bedroom. They will hold all your clothes with room to spare. The kitchen appliances are all new and the vinyl siding eliminates the need to paint. You won't have to put any money into this home for quite a while. The heating system has just been replaced and the energy costs are low because added insulation keeps the home energy efficient. I know you are concerned about yard work. The gardener that takes care of this property is willing to give the new owner a 25% discount for the next three years. That will save you a lot of money. Also, remember that our buyer protection plan covers you for any unexpected defects during the first year."

That real estate agent used his or her knowledge of what was important to you and then presented the features and benefits they represented. Everything was presented in a positive way. Here is a feature and the benefit it represents. This type of presentation helps remove doubt from the customer's mind.

Always present your solution from the positive point of view. Statements such as, "What I'd like to do is replace that product for you right now." Are positive in nature. Always avoid the use of any negative words such as can't won't, not, etc.

These words will not be accepted by your customer in a positive fashion. Negative words will cause the customer to become less receptive to your solution and point of view.

Never apologize for your solutions! Apologizing for your solution to the problem is a sure path to failure. If you apologize for your solutions, you are telling the customer that you don't think the resolution is fair. If you are telling him that, what chance do you have that the customer will be happy with your solution? If you start of by saying, "I'm sorry, but the best I can is.......", how do you think people will react. As soon as your customer hears the apology, they will react with negativity and come out of their comfort zone. When this happens, they will become less receptive and you will have lost ground in your attempts to resolve the problem.

Stage 6:

Making the Customer

Part of the Process

Do you want to hit a home run with your customer? Do you want to let your customer help you in the process? One very effective technique is to involve your customer in the decision making process. By making your customer part of the process, you increase the likelihood that the customer will be happy with the outcome.

Let's say you have two or more possible solutions that have approximately the same costs associated with them. Any of these solutions can resolve the issue and cost the company the same. It is up to you which solution to pick. In cases like these, enlist the help of the customer.

Present the solutions in the following way: "Sir, there are several things we can do. Let's discuss them and determine which one is the best for you. First, I can replace the defective product for you right now. We can check it out before you leave the store to insure that it is working properly. Second, you can pick out another comparable product and I can do an exchange. If you are not comfortable with your current product, that may be the way to go. Last, but not least, I can refund your money. I do know our prices are the best and you will spend more elsewhere but a refund is possible if you desire."

By letting your customer take part in the decision, you have allowed him or her to address every little issue that is in their mind. They can address issues you may never be aware of in a million years! They will also be more comfortable with any decision that they have had an active part in.

I do not want to sound like a broken record but we are still talking about that "comfort zone", in your customers mind. By allowing the customer to take part in the decision making process, you help create a huge comfort zone! Why do you think that is? What better way to create a comfort zone than to allow the customers to pick the resolution themselves? Who better to understand their own needs! If the customer cannot be comfortable with their own decisions, whose decisions can they be comfortable?

Another reason to allow the customer to participate in the process is that it provides the customer with an outlet for his frustrations. It also creates an impression of respect for the customer and a sincere desire to resolve the situation in a win-win manner.

Anything that helps reduce frustration, aids in the resolution process, and reduces the costs involved is a valuable tool in your service recovery toolbox. The effectiveness of these tools lies in your ability to use them correctly.

Stage 7:

Negotiating for Customer Satisfaction!

An important part of the service recovery process is negotiation. Negotiation is the art of give and take between two parties until both are satisfied with the result.

In service recovery, the customer is negotiating for the best possible resolution. You are negotiating for the satisfaction of the customer and their continued patronage. If you can reach a successful resolution, both parties will be satisfied.

As we have said previously, never present you best solution to the customer first. Always hold something back to use in negotiations. Negotiation requires that both sides have something to bargain with.

For the customer, it will be the willingness to drop one of their requests if you add something to your solution. For your part, it will be the addition of something of value to your original proposal. The process continues until both parties become satisfied or reach an impasse.

An example of a good negotiation would be: "I will give you a free upgrade instead of extending the warranty. Warranty extension is out of our control but the upgrade is something I can do for you." In this situation, the customer has requested something (the extended warranty) and you have countered with another offer (the free upgrade). If the offer is acceptable, both parties will reach a win-win solution. If there is still disagreement, the customer will make a counter offer.

In a counter offer, the other party will not agree to the original offer but instead offer something different. In the above example, the customer would say something like, "I realize that you can't increase the warranty but the free upgrade doesn't address my concerns. Could we exchange this product for another brand that comes with a longer warranty?" Here the customer has presented another possible resolution. You can either agree or make a counter proposal. The process continues until the issue is resolve or an impasse occurs.

It should be stated that effective negotiation requires give and take on both parties. If one party refuses to give up anything in return for your concessions, the whole process becomes futile. Here is an example of poor faith negotiations:

"I know you want the more expensive product for the same price. That is something out of my control. What I can do is offer you a 10% discount on that product instead." The customer replies, "That is not acceptable. I want the more expensive product for the same price and a free accessory thrown in." You reply, "I'll increase the discount to 15%, that's the best I can do." Your customer replies, "I want the expensive product for the same price, a free accessory thrown in, free delivery and set-up, a warranty extension, and a letter of apology from you and the store management."

In this case, you are making a sincere effort to resolve the issue but the customer is not negotiating in good faith. You are making concessions while the customer keeps increasing his or her demands until they get to a ridiculous level. When this occurs, an impasse is inevitable.

Always keep in mind that customers will always ask for more than they expect to get. Just as you hold back things to negotiate with, the customer will add demands on to his original request so that he has something to give up during negotiations.

It's kind of like a game where both parties try to see how much they can walk away from the situation with. There is nothing wrong with this as long as both parties come away satisfied.

The desired result should be the satisfaction of both parties. If one of the parties leaves the dispute feeling taken advantage of, the solution was not an effective one. Each side should negotiate until both parties have a solution they can live with.

How far should I go during negotiations?

Everyone should enter a negotiation with a clear understanding of just how far they can, and should, go with their proposed solutions. The cost of the negotiated solution will depend on the cost of the product purchased, the amount of products the customer purchases, and the value of future purchases that customer is expected to make.

We have talked about the importance of knowing the value of your customers. This information is invaluable on deciding just how much your are willing to offer during negotiations. Without this knowledge, you may offer a solution that will cost your company more than it will ever recoup in future purchases. This is not a win-win situation.

A good basis for negotiating solutions is to not exceed the profit generated by the original purchase.

For example, if a customer purchases a product for $100.00 and it costs the company $50.00, then the profit is $50.00. If the customer has a problem, and you can resolve it for $30.00, then your company still made $20.00 on the transaction. In this case you have a profit reduction but a little is better than nothing. This is why a solution is better than a refund. If the solution is going to cost more than the profit, sometimes a refund is a better alternative.

During negotiations, it is important that you take into consideration future reoccurrence of the same problem.

You may not wish to offer a requested solution because of the impact on similar situations in the future. For example, if you have a known problem with a product, a generous offer to one customer now may come back to haunt you in the future. If other customers hear of this offer, they may request the exact same settlement for their problem. Since every settlement has a cost associated with it, make certain that you can safely offer the solution to everyone with the same situation in the future.

If you cannot successfully negotiate an acceptable solution, do not be bullied into offering a solution that is not acceptable to you or your company. When this occurs, it is called an impasse. An impasse is a situation where a mutually acceptable situation cannot be achieved.

Stage 8:

Dealing with an

Impasse!

Up to this point, we have dealt with situations that could be resolved with a minimum of trouble. We were able to agree with the customer on the action taken and the result was a win-win situation. We used negotiation as a tool to protect the interest of all parties involved. What do we do when we just cannot resolve the issues?

There will be instance where you just cannot give the customer what he or she wants. The demands may be too high, the situation does not call for that particular action, or legal requirements stand in the way of resolving the issues. Whatever the reason, we must deal with the situation and bring the matter to a close one way or the other.

If there is disagreement between you and someone else in the company regarding this situation, make sure that you have your conversations in a private place, out of the range of the customers. You do not want to air your "dirty laundry" in front of others. The important objective here is to present a united front to your customers. Any hint of disagreement shifts the power over the situation in the customers' favor.

Do your best to be a calming presence in the situation. No matter how heated the exchanges may get, always stay cool and attempt to reduce the frustration level of the customer. Always keep in mind that the lower the frustration level, the easier and cheaper it will be to resolve the situation and satisfy the customer. If you find yourself getting to the point where you cannot keep your emotions in check, escalate the situations to someone else or excuse yourself for a minute and go somewhere to regroup your thoughts.

The first step is to determine why the situation cannot be resolved. Is it a legal issue? Is the situation not your responsibility but the customer refuses to admit that? Is it some other reason? Understanding the reasons behind an impasse enables you to determine what the next step is.

Escalation

There is not a person on this earth that can please every customer and get along with every person.

People are individual in nature and have their own strengths and weaknesses.

Very often, one person can succeed where others have failed in the past. Because of this, it is important to have an **escalation procedure.**

An escalation procedure is a procedure that directs problems to specific people when the first contact is unable to resolve the issue. (Notice I did not say fail to resolve it. Unsuccessful efforts are not failures. Anything done to reduce the frustration level of the customer is a successful effort.) An example of an escalation procedure would be:

Step 1:	Supervisor
Step 2:	Department Manager
Step 3:	Middle Manager
Step 4:	Division Vice-President
Step 5:	President

Legal Issues:	Attorney's Office
Shipping Issues:	Warehouse Supervisor
Accounting:	Sr. Account Manager

The purpose of the escalation procedure is to have an outlet for unresolved issues. Knowing who to assign the unresolved issue to enables the customer to have another option to resolve the issue. For example, if you have done everything you can do and are unable to resolve an issue, you would transfer the customer to the next person on the escalation list.

Usually that person will have more authority and will be able to offer a better resolution if that is the right thing to do. In any case, escalation is the best option.

In some cases, there will be more than one person in the same position as you. In these situations, just transferring the customer to another person may do the trick. Sometimes just transferring the customer to another employee of a different gender will help a great deal. It may be that the customer feels more at ease talking with a woman or a man whatever the case may be. Always keep in mind that the desired end result is customer satisfaction.

We have talked in detail about policies and procedures. We have stressed the need for uniform enforcement by all people in the company. There is no important area for this than service recovery.

In service recovery, we are attempting to recover from a bad or negative experience. It is critical that everything be handled without further inconvenience. Having a written procedure will enable the customer to be transferred to the correct person every time. Without this procedure, the results can be disastrous!

Using Escalation to Resolve Issues

You have done everything you can and cannot resolve the problem. You have determined the correct person on the escalation list.

The next thing you do is to transfer the customer to that person. Before you do that, there are two things that must be done.

The first thing is to give the customer the name, title, and number of the person that you are going to transfer them to. This way, if the customer should get disconnected, they can call back direct and not have to go through you again. This creates a certain comfort level and will reduce resolution time.

The second thing you should do is to put the customer on hold while you give a BRIEF background of the situation to the person that the customer will be talking to next. This accomplishes two things. First, it gives you an opportunity to provide relevant background information on the specific situation. The person will know what has been done up to that point, the offers that were made, and what the customer is looking for from the company.

The second thing this accomplishes is that it provides the person with an opportunity to formulate his or her own strategy for dealing with the situation. The worst possible thing to have happen is for the new person to pick up the phone cold and have to have the customer start from square one.

Providing background also eliminates the customer from putting words in your mouth. If you have told the person you offered a 15% discount and the customer says you offered them a 50% discount, the new person will have the facts available to them.

One important thing about transferring customers. Always make the call for them. Do NOT tell them to call back and ask for Mr. Jones at ext. 345.

This creates more work for the customer and increases his or her frustration level. Always keep in mind that we want to do everything we can to reduce the frustration level of the customer. Always make the customer do as little as possible.

If the person on the escalation list is not available, you have two choices. If there is a second person designated to take the calls then you can transfer them to the second person. If there is no second person, tell the customer that the person is not available at the moment and inform the customer that the person will call the customer back within a certain time period.

NOTE: There should be a company policy in place for promising a return phone call within a certain time frame. Adhere to that policy. It is better to give the customer a longer time frame and have the call come sooner than to give a small time frame and have the call come late.

Establishing a time frame sets a certain level of expectation. Once the time frame is stated the call must be made within that time frame or your credibility takes a real nosedive.

Whenever something is escalated, there should be a record made of the situation. This record is nothing more than an accounting of what was said, when it was said, and whom it was said to.

If your company has a computerized customer service system, this record should be indexed in that customer file.

This record enables others to determine what has happened to date without having to contact you for the information. Records help streamline the information gathering process and reduce resolution time. We all know the importance of that!

Another reason for records is that they provide a legal accounting of what has transpired. Should the customer take you to court, the records can be introduced as evidence.

WARNING: Records and documents can be introduced in court. Refrain from adding personal comments and observations into these records. Statements such as "customer is a moron" or:"don't offer this jerk anything" can come back to haunt you. In addition, refrain from writing anything in documents that directly refers to a known product defect or admission of guilt or responsibility.

One more word about escalation. Do not consider the need to escalate an issue as an admission of failure. Consider it a good judgement and an act of good faith on the behalf of your customer. You will do more good, and have a greater level of customer satisfaction, if you recognize the need for escalation and take advantage of it. There will be many cases where you will be called upon to resolve a problem someone else couldn't.

Think about what would happen if you don't escalate an issue. You have three alternatives.

You give in and give more than you should. The customer gives up and goes somewhere else in the future. You continue to talk and talk for hours, saying the same things over and over again, and accomplish nothing. You tell me, who is the failure, the person that escalates, or the person that let's their pride get in the way and refuses to accept help.

Escalation is just another tool in your service recovery toolbox. Use it to your customer's advantage. It will increase customer satisfaction and reduce your amount of job related stress. Sounds like a win-win situation doesn't it?

Stage 9:

The Impossible

Situation

It is important to realize that you are going to have situations where it is just not possible to satisfy the customer no matter how high you escalate and how much you offer. There are always some people that are just going to keep asking for more and more and never be satisfied.

There are also going to be situations that are out of your control. It may be that your product was installed incorrectly and there is nothing you can do. Maybe your customer purchased a product that is not intended to be used like they are using it. These situations are not resolvable. What do you do in these situations?

The one thing you must never, ever do, is promise something that you can't deliver just to make the problem disappear for a while. This is a sure recipe for disaster.

Promising things you can't deliver will send the frustration level of your customer through the roof. Always consider that you may be the one to talk to this customer the next time he calls. How would you defend your empty promises? If you can't, who else could?

The important thing to realize is that you must make options available to the customer. If the product is installed wrong, don't just tell the customer that and hang up. Offer to send the customer installation instructions. Provide the customer with the name and number of someone who can reinstall it correctly. Taking the time to give options to the customer shows that you care about the problem and are willing to spend the extra time to help resolve it. The more options you can provide the customer, the happier that customer will be.

Always remain polite and friendly no matter how ugly the situation gets. The last thing you want to do is make a bad situation even worse by getting into an altercation with a customer. Some customers will do their best to provoke you into a shouting match and then turn around and use your statements against you. Always remember that some customers will always remember that they were totally innocent and you were abusive towards them for no reason at all. Don't give them any more ammunition than they may already have.

It is not possible to achieve 100% customer satisfaction and still respect the interests of the company. We cannot give everything away, every day, and still remain profitable.

Because of this, it is important to set realistic goals. Depending on your industry, your customer satisfaction goals may be 99% or 90%. Always take into consideration the situations that are out of your control and factor them into the equation when setting your customer satisfaction goals. If you can satisfy a customer in one of those impossible situations by providing options and / or service to them, that's great.

Take steps to improve processes and actions that are within your control. For those situations out of your control, try and identify actions and methods to reduce or minimize their occurrence. You should concentrate your efforts, and funds, on those customers that you can help, Always take into consideration the value of that customer and the future ramifications of your actions. Remember, what you give away today, you may also have to give away tomorrow.

Taking It Personally

One of the most common obstacles to overcome is the feeling that arguments and dissatisfaction are aimed at you personally. With rare exceptions, the customer doesn't know you from anyone else in the company. You just happen to be the person that individual wound up talking to at that point in time.

The frustrations your customer feels are not because of you but rather the entire company, or the product that it sold.

These frustrations are being taken out on you because you are the individual that the person is talking with. Never lose sight of that.

See the customers' words and emotions for what they are. The results of past experiences and frustrations. Do whatever you can to turn the situation around. Stay cheerful and try to be helpful. If you feel that you can no longer be effective in dealing with that individual, escalate the situation. Think of escalation as your safety net. Use it when you must.

Never feel that you have failed when you cannot resolve an issue. It is not a personal failure when you turn a problem over to someone else. Instead, think of it as an action designed to improve your company's chances of retaining that customer. Remember that you are part of a team and that individual successes and failures are secondary to the success or failure of the team. Always do your best for the team.

People in the service industry are held to high standards. To generate and maintain a satisfaction rating of 90% or higher, you must make 90 out of every 100 people happy! That is not an easy task. In professional baseball, for example, the premier hitter still fails over 60% of the time! How long do you think your company would last if your customer satisfaction rating were less than 40%? Not very long, I'm sure!

In service recovery programs, the task is much harder.

Not only are you expected to maintain, or even improve, your customer satisfaction, the cases you handle will be cases that already have significant negative experiences attached to them. This makes the process that much more difficult.

The point that I am trying to make here is that you cannot expect yourself to solve every single problem that comes across your counter or desk. This does not mean that you don't give 110% of yourself for each customer, it means that sometimes even the best efforts are not enough to satisfy the customer. Give it your best and accept the results. Don't take failure personally and don't allow a negative experience to effect the next person you deal with. This is what it takes to be a professional and to represent your company the way it needs to be represented.

Stage 10:

Acknowledging the Resolution

If you are fortunate to get to the point of resolving the issue in a satisfactory manner, the next step is for all parties to acknowledge the resolution.

Very often, a resolution is the result of several conversations with multiple parties. In the course of negotiations, there were many offers and counter offers. To insure that everyone agrees on the same resolution, we must restate everything agrees upon to this point. Simply going over the resolution with the customer one more time does this. Here is an example:

"I'm glad we were able to resolve this problem for you Mr., Ryan. I'd just like to recap what we have agreed on. We will replace the product for you and extend the warranty to compensate you for the time lost to date. We will deliver it free of charge on Thursday November 12 in the morning since you work in the afternoon hours. In exchange, you agree to pay your account in full within 10 business days. Is this correct or have I missed anything?"

This accomplishes several things. First, it gives the customer one final opportunity to accept or decline the offer. Second, it makes the customer part of the resolution process. Third, it gives the customer one final opportunity to bring up any issues that may still remain to be addressed. Lastly, it helps bring closure to the issue. Closure, as discussed previously, lets your customer accept the situation as complete.

This recap also provides an important purpose for your company. It allows you one last check against future problems. Since we do not want any additional negative experiences, we must make sure that there is no misunderstanding or miscommunication up to this point. If the customer thinks they are entitled to one thing, and you think your are providing something else, what do you think the effect is going to be on customer satisfaction? It would be a shame to have all the hard work done up to this point wasted because someone wanted to save two minutes talking to the customer.

Stage 11: Going One Step Further!

Now that you have resolved the issue and satisfied the customer, how would you like to do one simple thing that will send you customer satisfaction rating through the roof? I would assume the answer is yes!

After you resolve the issue, and your customer has agreed to the resolution, offer your customer something extra for their time and inconvenience! It doesn't have to be something expensive. The amount will be dependant on the amount of the product involved and that particular customer. The important thing is to show your customers that you appreciate their business.

There are two things that every person in the world likes. Something for free and to be appreciated. Why not combine the two and hit a customer service homerun!

Your options can be unlimited. Send your customers two free passes to the local Movie Theater. Send them a fruit or candy basket. How about a considerable discount on their next purchase? Anything that has a value to your customers will be appreciated. (NOTE: Avoid offering your customers something that is intended to make them spend more money with your business. Customers will see through these offers and will be offended by them. If you offer a discount off a future purchase, be sure an make it a good one.)

Present the offer after all negotiations are done. You want this offer to stand on its own and represent your company's appreciation for this customer. If you make it part of the settlement, it will appear to just be something else that was negotiated. Present the offer like this:

"Mr. Smith, I'm glad we were able to resolve this problem for you. I will see that everything is taken care of. We do appreciate your business. I would like to send you two free movie tickets as a token of our appreciation. They will arrive within two weeks. I hope you will enjoy the movie. Thank you very much for your patience. Have a great day1"

What do you think the response from the customer is going to be? In 99.9% of the cases it will be extremely positive. You have accomplished two important things.

First, you have shown the customer that you care about them and appreciate their business. This is what all customers want. Second, you have ended the entire process on a very positive note. This is the last experience in your customers' mind. It will carry a lot of weight in forming the new perception of your company. What is that worth to you and your company? Probably a lot more than two movie tickets!

Giving your customers something extra after everything is done is yet another tool in your service recovery toolbox. Use it correctly and you'll hit a customer service homerun every time!

Stage 12:
Follow Up, Follow Up, Follow Up!

Up to now, all our efforts have been focused on identifying a solution that would both satisfy the customer and keep the interest of the company intact. That's not always easy. If you can accomplish that, and you must, you must make sure that everything promised is delivered on time and in the manner that it was promised.

If there are several things that need to happen, make sure that all the people involved know exactly what it is they must do in a particular situation. Provide each person with the exact task that must be done. Include dates, special instructions, and any other information necessary to insure that the correct things are done in the proper time frame.

After this is all done, you're finished, right. Of course, you have negotiated a solution that makes everyone happy, and you have made everyone aware of what needs to be done. Your job is done.

Not really. The last step you should take separates the winners from the losers. After everything has been done, and everything has been delivered to the customer as promised, follow up with the customer.

Give them a call and make sure they received what they were promised. Make sure they are happy. This creates a wonderful feeling of confidence and security in the minds of your customers. We want to re-establish that "comfort zone" that existed before the problem came up. We want your customers to think of you and your company when the time for their next purchase comes. We want your customers to think, "You know, I was treated very well when I had that problem last year. That's a great company to do business with!" If you can get those feelings in your customer's mind, you're a winner!

There may be times when this follow up phone call will result in additional problems being brought to your attention. The vast majority of the time, you will just be thanked for your concern. If trouble does pop up, aren't you better off finding out rather than losing the customer? Always remember that problems are opportunities to show your customers just how good you can be!

Another effective technique is to use satisfaction surveys to find out what your customer really felt about the experience. These surveys are more accurate because some people are intimidated when talking with someone on the phone and may not give their true feelings. Survey results also give you feedback on just what part of the process was accepted and what parts were not. Choose your questions carefully. Questions should be used to pinpoint each part of the service process. If you do a mail survey, include a postage paid return envelope. It will increase the number of people that will send the survey back.

Surveys, whether written or verbal, are only as useful as the way the data is used. You can mail out the best surveys in the world, but if you do nothing with the data, the survey is useless. Use the data to improve procedures and policies. Keep yourself constantly changing to make things better for your customers. Your competition is doing it, I promise you. You better d it too!

When It's All Over!

When the dust settles, and you have averted another disaster, plucked that lost customer back from the clutches of the competition, and restored his or her faith in your company, it's time to take a look back.

It's time to pat yourself on the back and take pride in a job well done. It's also time to look back and see the time and effort that was put in to resolving an issue. It's also a good time to see if the problem could have been avoided in the first place.

Service Recovery is hard work. Don't let anyone tell you otherwise. It can be stressful and frustrating at times. It can also be very rewarding. The focus on service recovery should also be placed on identifying problems that have occurred and taking steps to eliminate future occurrences.

If you work hard to resolve a problem, but do nothing about seeing that the problem doesn't reoccur, what exactly have you accomplished?

You may have saved a customer but you have done nothing about other customers that may have the same problems in the future.

Have Regularly Scheduled Meetings

One very effective technique is to hold regular meetings were various situations are reviewed and discussed. If certain situations are shown to occur over and over, studies should be made to determine the source of the problem.

If a few situations were very troublesome, they should be reviewed step by step to determine why they were so difficult and whether they should be handled differently in the future. In customer service, and service recovery, we learn from our mistakes. Policies and procedures are never written in stone. They can, and should, be changed and updated regularly. Keep what remains effective and change what is no longer working.

Use the input of everyone from the top to the bottom. Sales clerks, warehouse people, drivers, and installers are the employees closest to the customer. Don't underestimate the value of their knowledge and input.

Share Success!

We are all too quick to point out the bad things that happen in our company and in our lives.

Very few people stop to compliment people on a job well done.

If someone has done a good job, acknowledge it! Have that person share what he or she had done. Recognition is a positive motivator and others will learn how to react in similar situations. Customer Service and Service Recovery are team efforts. The success of the team is dependent on the actions of the team members. This does not mean that individual efforts should not be rewarded or recognized. If you have any doubts about this ask yourself one question. If someone on a team makes a bad mistake, would you fire the entire team? No. You would fire that individual. Don't' you think recognition could, and should, work the same way? Think about it.

Handling Abuse

There are going to be times when you are confronted with some type of abuse. Abuse can be emotional, physical, or verbal in nature. It is important that your company has a policy on dealing with abuse. Various types of abuse are blatantly illegal and should be dealt with as such. Other types require a company policy on how to deal with those situations.

Physical abuse deals with bodily abuse such as pushing, shoving, or more violent behavior. This type of abuse should never be tolerated. In these cases it is best to leave the area or call a manager or co-worker to come to your aid. Never return any physical abuse. Leave the area first. While there may be exceptions to this rule, it is a safe resolution to the immediate problem. Check with your company for specific policy and procedure.

Verbal abuse is the most common form of abuse. Verbal abuse is the result of a very high level of frustration.

The frustration results in an emotional outburst. When this occurs, remain a calming presence. Try to get the customer to calm down and reduce their frustration level. If this does not work, use a phrase similar to "I really want to help you but your language is really limiting what I can do for you, sir." If the verbal abuse continues, inform the customer that you are terminating the conversation if the abuse does not stop. If the customer continues, politely hand up the phone or leave the immediate area. Inform your supervisor or manager of the incident. We all know the customer is going to call back, or speak to someone else. Get your side of the incident known to your immediate supervisor.

Emotional abuse may take the form of threats or intimidation. Depending on the severity of the statements or actions, take the appropriate actions. Consult your manager or supervisor immediately and have the incident recorded. Again, be sure to follow all established policies and procedures for dealing with these situations.

Taking abuse is not in any person's job description. It is, however, part of the customer service person's job from time to time. When these situations occur, try and reduce the frustration level and understand that the customer is feeling very frustrated with the situation. He or she may have been unable to resolve this issue for a long time. They may have spoken to many people that did not do anything to help them. You are the person that is getting the result of everyone else's actions.

Be understanding, reduce the frustration level, and do your best to resolve the situation. That is all you can do. If these efforts to not help the situation, escalate the situation to someone else, or politely terminate the conversation.

It is also important that you take a minute or two after one of these incidents to calm down and get yourself back to a neutral state. Once hazard of abuse is that it can follow you to the next customer. Never allow the previous experience to dictate how you will treat the next customer. Your next customer deserves your very best. You can only give them your best when you are at your best.

Managing Service

Recovery!

Now that we have a program designed, and everyone is trained on how to resolve customer service problems, how do we operate the program? Who should run the program? What is the right, and wrong, way to manage Service Recovery programs?

Service Recovery programs are administrated in much the same way that Customer Service and Service departments are run. You develop procedures and policies and have someone in place to monitor performance, oversee employees, and take responsibility for the financial end of the business. There is one very important distinct, however, when it comes to managing Service Recovery.

The person managing a Service Recovery program must have confidence in those working for him or her.

The manager must allow employees to be free thinkers allowed to work within a specific set of guidelines. The manager must be a motivator that enforces company rules, procedures, and goals while at the same time remain focused on customer satisfaction.

Service Recovery is no place for a micro-management style of managing. For those of you that are not familiar with the term, micro-management means managing employees down to the most minute tasks. Micro managers allow little or no freethinking and require their employees get management approval on every decision. In Service Recovery, this means large increases in resolution time, more time spent on each customer which means less customer get served each day, and extremely poor customer service.

The ideal manager for a Service Recovery program is a manager that is focused on customer service. He or she knows the importance of quality customer service and its effects on sales and profits. The manager should be very self-assured and not afraid to allow decisions to be made by those in his department.

The ideal manager allows his or her people to make mistakes. He provides guidelines in which to work. If an employee goes outside those guidelines in a special set of circumstances, he will discuss the matter and make a decision about how that same situation will be handled in the future.

The Most Important Management Tool in Service Recovery!

When I was in service management, I told those working for me that a true measure of how effective I was as a manager was how things ran when I was away for an extended period of time. When I was not there to make a decision, what would happen? Would someone else make the decision, or would things come to an abrupt halt?

Independent thinking is the heart and soul of all customer service and service recovery efforts. Independent thinking resolves issues quickly and effectively.

Customer satisfaction soars and problems go away quickly and easily. If you can get your employees to think independently, you have half your battle won!

How do you get your employees to think independently? The first thing you need to do is get your employees to stop being afraid to make a mistake. The number one obstacle of thinking independently is the fear of reprisal when a mistake is made. If people are yelled at or chastised when they make a simple mistake, you will never get employees to think on their own.

When you first start trying to get people to think on their own, you will get a lot of skepticism from your employees. The will be leery of your motives and probably will be hesitant to make their own decisions. The only remedy is to build trust between employees and management.

An effective way to build trust is to talk to your employees as a group and tell them exactly what you want them to do. What is the focus of their actions? What is the goal of the department or team? What needs to happen to achieve that goal? Make them part of the program. Give them a felling that their viewpoints and skills are vital to the long-term success of the program.

When they are in a group, give them a set of guidelines regarding making decisions. Let them know that they are to make the decisions on all resolutions within these guidelines.

Make it clear that you do NOT want to be consulted on decisions that fall between these guidelines. If there are unusual circumstances, have your employees make the decisions. Encourage them to think on their own.

Depending on your situation, you can start out with very small guidelines. For example, you can start out new employees by saying they are authorized t approve resolutions which cost less than $50.00. After they get a little experience, raise the limit to $100.00 or $200.00. The idea is to have as many issues resolved on the spot as possible.

Mistakes will happen. It is how you handle them that counts. If someone acts within the guidelines and makes a decision that is against your policy, do not chastise or berate that individual. Instead, meet with that person in private and discuss the situation. It is possible there were circumstances which justified the particular course of action. If so, praise the action taken. If the decision was wrong, take the time to explain why you would have taken a different approach and why. The idea is for the employee to gain an understanding of how things should be done. If you take the time to talk about these situations, employees will know how to react when a similar situation comes up again.

If you react positively to these incidents, you do not cause your employees to fear making mistakes.

Instead, your employees will gain an increased understanding in what you and your company expects them to do. They will improve their efficiency and increase customer satisfaction. That is the end result of all your service recovery efforts.

An effective service recovery manager listens to his or her people. The people that interact with the customers every day are closer to the problems than just about anyone in the company. They have the pulse of the company available to them on a daily basis. A good manager realizes this and uses this information effectively.

The ideal Service Recovery manager must be a strong and self-confident person. He must show support to his or her people and be a model of what customer service is all about. The manager must stand behind his employees when they make the right decision and the situation gets worse. There is nothing more frustrating than an employee who follows procedures and policies, makes all the right decisions and then is left to take the heat when things go bad.

A good manager also realizes that his or her best assets are the employees. A machine or computer cannot show compassion, reduce frustration, and talk a customer out of going to the competition. A good manager also knows that some skills just can't be measured in dollars and sense. A mind capable of being inventive and creative is worth its weight in gold in customer service.

Last, but not least, a good Service Recovery manager fights to make things better. A good manager sees continuing problems as a drain on their resources. A good manager realizes the need for praise for a job well done. A pat on the back, or recognition in front of their peers is a powerful management tool. A good manager, like a good carpenter or mechanic, knows how to use all the tools in their toolbox.

Conclusion

There's been a lot of information here that you have read. Some of it may appear to be common sense. Some of it may appear to be trivial. The point is, even the largest project is made up of small steps. You can't accomplish something involved without implementing the basics.

Service Recovery should not be viewed as a project or department that loses money. While it is true that solutions cost the company money, the retention of the customer saves the company far greater amounts over time. Any company can act nice when you buy something. It's when a problem arises that you find out which companies you can count on.

Service Recovery speaks out to your customers.

It says, "We care!" It delivers the message, "We appreciate your business!" It also tells your competition that you're a force to be reckoned with.

Your efforts in proper service recovery techniques will pay handsome dividends. Service Recovery doesn't cost, it pays.

"Hidden" Benefits of Service Recovery Skills

Working in Customer Service is a very demanding, and sometimes very stressful, occupation. It requires patience, understanding, compassion, and a thorough knowledge of products, policies, and procedures. All of these items then are used to form an approach that must differ from person to person in order to be effective.

How simple it would be if we could create a manual that would tell us how to react in every possible situation. Whoever could produce such a manual would be a multi-millionaire almost over night! Unfortunately, no one has developed a single approach that satisfies every human mind.

A formal Service Recovery program reduces stress levels in the workplace. It provides options and outlets to people who don't know where to turn next. A good service recovery program makes the work environment more relaxed and more confident.

The more confident and relaxed a person is, the better they perform. The less stress in a person's job, the longer he or she will remain in that position.

Less stress also means less employee turnover. How frustrating it is when we spend time and money training a person and, just when they get really good at their job, they leave to work somewhere else. The losses a company incurs in these situations are huge. Any steps that can be taken to reduce employee turnover will reduce costs, and improve efficiency and morale.

I can't expect anyone to understand why people in customer service do what they do. There are far more glamorous professions. There are higher paying professions. There must be other reasons.

I can say that the feeling that comes from satisfying another human being is a pretty good feeling. When you can have that feeling every day of the week, there's something to be said for that. Being able to take an unhappy customer and make him want to come back again and again is like hitting a homerun. It takes hard work but anything that's worth anything takes work.

The one really great thing about customer service skills is that they are transferable. Making a customer happy uses the same skills that we use to make our spouses and friends happy. Listening skills, for example, are used in just about every facet of our lives. What better reason to learn your customer service skills.

Take the time to learn your skills. Start small and build your skills on a solid foundation. You will soon see results. Your skills will improve and take your career to new heights. Your communication skills will improve and help you in every area of your life, not only in the workplace.

Last but not least, you will improve yourself. Every day you will be just a little bit better than you were the day before. Success is not gained in leaps and bounds but rather through a series of small steps. Start taking those steps. Take them one at a time. Those steps will add up and take you a very long way. I wish you luck on your journey. A special journey that leaves a trail of satisfied customers and smiling faces. I think I understand now.

For more information on Customer Service Training, please go to:

http://www.customerservicetraininginstitute.com